Luka,

As you grow older, play hard,
play fair and stay safe!
Do A Lover You & your family!

Happy Birthday!!!

Chukemi Akunne
02 22 2020

To: Grandpa and Grandma, MA and the 3Ds

First Edition
Copyright ©2017 by Olukemi Akinrinola
All rights reserved.
Published by Lighthouse Press, Agape Inc

For information regarding permission, write to:
The Lighthouse,15600 E. Caley Pl, Centennial,
CO 80016.

ISBN-13:978-0-9994012-2-4.

Visit us at www.itsecus.com

Printed in the USA

Book description:

Children love to play in playgrounds. Monkey bars, swings, see-saws and other playground attractions give them a sense of freedom and excitement as they push themselves to the limits of their young bodies.

But occasionally there are accidents.

I Got a Pink Cast is a book for children that tells the true story of one such playground accident, when a little girl falls from the monkey bars at her school and breaks her arm.

It details the pain and initial shock, followed by a visit to the hospital, x-rays, the placing of a cast on the injury and the road to recovery. With colorful images and a relevant and important message running throughout, **I Got a Pink Cast** is a cautionary tale of the dangers that can be found in the unlikeliest of places.

My name is Janet and I love to jump on Monkey bars.

I also love to do cart wheels and have fun in the playground.

This book is a true story.

I want other kids to learn and stay safe.

I have been waiting for April 18th! It is finally here and guess what?

It's my birthday!!! Everyone was happy for me. Yay, I am finally 5 years old!

7

The next day, my parents brought lots of cupcakes for my afternoon class in school.

My birthday celebration continues, whoohoo..but first, we all have to play in the playground after lunchtime and then, we will have some cupcakes.

I go to the slides and then to the monkey bars and oops, my hands slipped from the bar and I fell so hard ! I can't get up, it hurts so bad!!!!!!

Ouch!

I am crying in pain and my teachers help me to stand up but it hurts anytime I move. My left arm feels so different, the pain is not stopping!

I am really crying now, my teachers have put some ice on my arm but it hurts even more.

This is the worst pain I have ever had! My arm is getting bigger and why are my bones wiggly?

I can't move my fingers and I am so scared!

My teachers have called my mom and she is on her way.

One of my teachers gives me a pink lollipop and makes me sit down quietly.

Maybe, my mom will fix my arm because she is a doctor but she needs to fix the pain first.

It is hurting from the moon and back!

Soon, my mom gets to school and sees me crying, when she told me, I will be OK, I feel better a little bit but I have to move slowly so my arm does not hurt more.